Introduction to PET

Annette Capel

Rosemary Nixon

OXFORD

UNIVERSITY PRESS

Contents

Reading 1	Understanding notices and messages	4
	Understanding the meaning	
	Grammar **Imperatives**	
Speaking 1	Talking about yourself and your home	6
	Introducing yourself	
	Describing a picture	
Listening 1	Hearing about places	8
	Choosing between pictures	
	Grammar **Present tenses**	
	Hearing numbers and spelled words	
Writing 1	Thinking about your writing	10
	Spelling words correctly	
	Getting the grammar right	
	Checking word order	
	Correcting punctuation	

Using the *PET Masterclass* **Vocabulary reference 1** 12
    Topic vocabulary
    Verbs and nouns that go together

Using the *PET Masterclass* **Grammar reference 1** 13
    Grammar terminology
    Verbs in the past simple

Reading 2	**Making connections**	14
	Matching people to texts Fact or opinion? Grammar **Ability**	
Speaking 2	**Making choices**	16
	Making suggestions Agreeing and disagreeing Giving reasons Making decisions	
Listening 2	**Hearing about thoughts and feelings**	18
	Understanding people's opinions Grammar **Comparison**	
Writing 2	**Developing your writing**	20
	Writing longer sentences Showing vocabulary range Showing grammatical range	

Using the *PET Masterclass* **Vocabulary reference 2** — 22
Describing things

Using the *PET Masterclass* **Grammar reference 2** — 23
Grammar – form
Grammar – use

Reading 1 Understanding notices and messages

Warm up

1 Look around you. How many notices and signs can you see? What do they tell you?

Understanding the meaning

2 Read the short texts 1–5 and match them with the words.

text message   ~~email~~
postcard   telephone message
notice

1 *email* ....
2 ....
3 ....
4 ....
5 ....

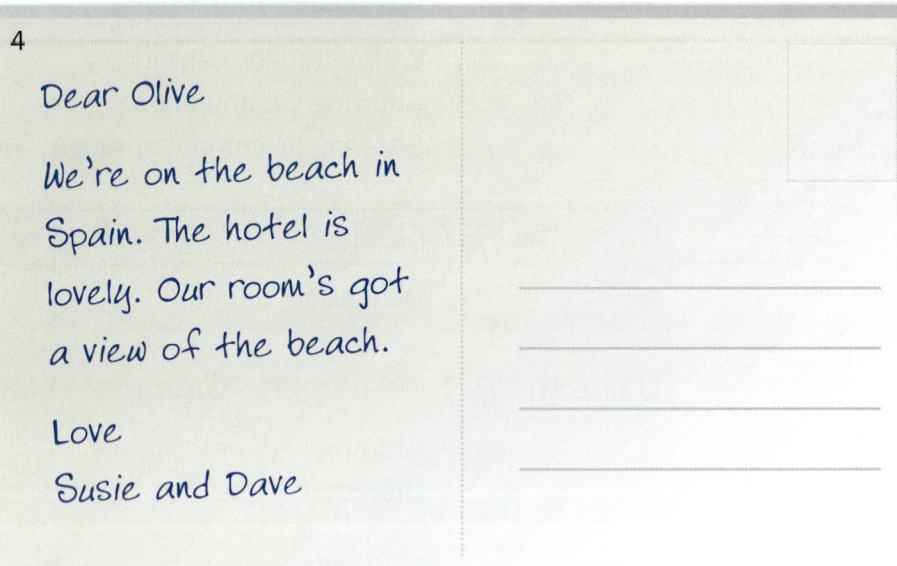

1
To: Ken
From: Jemma

Hi Ken
It's my birthday on Sunday. We're having a picnic in Victoria Park at 3p.m. Bring some food to share.

Love
Jemma

2
THIS IS
A QUIET AREA.
SWITCH OFF
MOBILE PHONES.

3
Do you want a lift tomorrow? I can pick you up at 8.30. Give me a ring – 07394 465007.
C U Phil

5
Your mum phoned. Please buy some bread, cheese and tomatoes on your way home.

4
Dear Olive

We're on the beach in Spain. The hotel is lovely. Our room's got a view of the beach.

Love
Susie and Dave

3 Match the notices and messages with the purposes on the right. There is one more than you need.

Text 1 ⎤ to ask someone to go shopping
Text 2 ⎦ to offer to drive somebody somewhere
           to invite someone to a party
Text 3   to give advice on what to do in an emergency
Text 4   to give an instruction telling you what to do
Text 5   to give news from a holiday

4 Which sentence (a or b) means the same as the text?

1. a Come to a party in the park and bring some food for everyone.
   b Get some food for yourself and meet friends in the park.
2. a Talk quietly on your mobile phone in this area.
   b You cannot use your mobile phone here.
3. a Kate should phone Phil to tell him if she wants a lift.
   b Phil will phone Kate at 8.30 to ask her if she wants a lift.
4. a Susie and Phil are writing in their room in the hotel.
   b Susie and Phil are staying at a nice hotel near the sea.
5. a Your mother is going shopping before she goes home.
   b You need to do some shopping on your journey home.

5 Underline the phrases in the texts which mean the same as phrases in the correct sentences in **4**. Circle words or phrases in the other sentence which have a different meaning.

Example

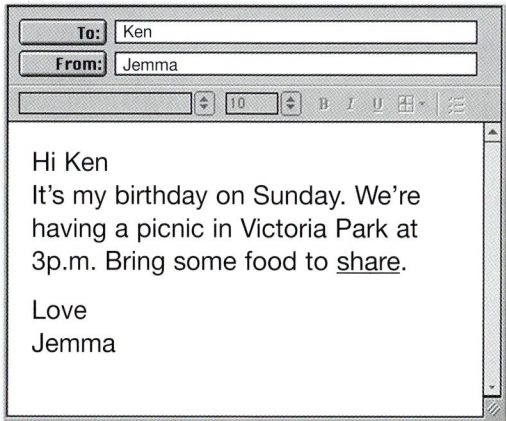

1. a Come to a party in the park and bring some food for <u>everyone</u>.
   b Bring a picnic lunch (for yourself) to eat with friends in the park.

● **PET Point**

In Reading Part 1 you need to understand the exact meaning of the message.

6 Put the sentences in the correct order to make one notice and one message.

Phone me to tell me the homework.
Use the stairs on the right.
Luke – I'm not coming to the lesson tomorrow.
Thanks, Henry.
This lift is out of order.

7 What do the texts in **6** say? Choose A, B or C for each.

1. A It is better to use the stairs than the lift.
   B You have to go up the stairs because the lift doesn't work.
   C Wait on the right for the lift to come.
2. Henry wants Luke to
   A give him the answers to the homework.
   B tell the teacher he won't be in class.
   C phone to tell him what the homework is.

Grammar

Imperatives

8 Underline the imperatives used in the notices and messages on page 4.

■ **Remember**

An imperative is used to give instructions, advice and warnings.

9 Use some of the imperatives you found in **8** to complete the notices.

1. .... all the lights when you leave the office.
2. .... your dictionaries to the next lesson.
3. .... me your car keys. I'll drive.
4. .... lots of food for dinner – I'm hungry!

10 Put the words in the correct order to make notices. Add the correct punctuation.

1. line behind the wait
2. animals feed the don't
3. ON DON'T BUS EAT THE
4. your leave keys reception at
5. form using complete a pen the black
6. closed this keep door
7. HANDS LEAVE YOUR BEFORE WASH YOU
8. two after every tablets take meal

Speaking 1 Talking about yourself and your home

Warm up

1 Work in pairs. Make a list of five situations when you might need to introduce yourself or explain who you are.

Introducing yourself

2 Listen to two people meeting and introducing themselves. Complete the information.

Man's name: ¹............................ Casey
From: ²............................, Australia

Woman's name: ³............................ Field
From: ⁴............................, England

3 Listen to the next part of the dialogue between Frank and Anna. Complete the table.

	Type of accommodation	Reason for living there	Job/occupation
Anna	house	cheaper to share	
Frank			

4 Where does Frank live? Listen again and write down the name of the place.

5 Introduce yourself to different people in the class. Ask each other about where you live and what type of home you have.

⬤ **PET Point**
In Speaking Part 1 the examiner will ask you questions about your daily life.

Describing a picture

6 Look at the photo of a living room. Read and listen to Louisa describing it. She makes five mistakes describing where things are. Find and underline them.

This is a picture of a living room. It looks quite big. On the left-hand side there's a big window. It has blinds on it. In front of the window there's a small sofa. In the foreground on the left there's another sofa – it's light brown. In front of this sofa is a lamp. In the middle of the room there's a low table. There are several things on it. I think there are some candles and a box. In the corner of the room there's a tall cupboard. It's opposite some shelves. There are some plants on the top of the cupboard. Then on the left-hand side, I can see a fire. Under the fire there's a picture – it's a picture of a house, or a shop.

7 Find phrases in the text in **6** to describe positions 1–3.

1 ……………..   2 ……………..   3 ……………..

8 There is one thing in the picture Louise forgets to talk about. What is it?

9 Work in pairs. Using the description in **6** to help you, describe the room in the picture below.

● **PET Point**
In Speaking Part 3 you have to describe a photograph.

10 In pairs, ask and answer the questions.
1 Which room do you prefer? Why?
2 Do you like modern or traditional furniture?
3 What's your home like? Describe the living room.

7

Listening 1 Hearing about places

Warm up

1 Work with a partner. Look carefully at the picture. For 1–6, decide what the missing things could be.

2 Now listen to the recording to check your ideas.

● **PET Point**
In Listening Part 1, you listen and choose your answers from sets of pictures.

Choosing between pictures

3 Match the words to each picture. What else can you see in each picture?

apartment   beach   floor   keys   pool
shelf   sofa   trees   ~~volleyball~~   window

1

  volleyball ....

2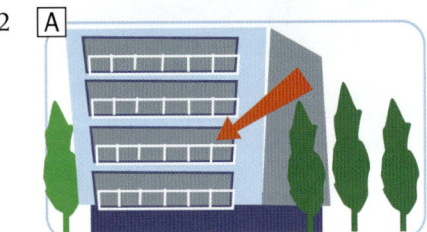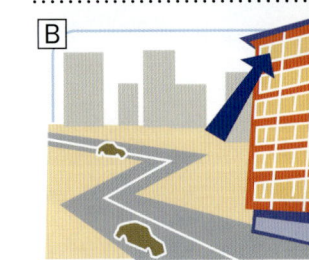

  ....

3

  ....

4 Choose a question from 1–6 that goes with both of the pictures in each set.
  1 Where are the woman's keys?
  2 Which swimming pool do they decide to go to?
  3 Who is living in the second floor apartment?
  4 What is Tomas doing this afternoon?
  5 Where does Jane live now?
  6 What is on the bookshelf?

5 Now listen to the recording for the first set of pictures. Think about the question and choose A or B.

Hearing numbers and spelled words

⦿ **PET Point**
In Listening Part 3, you need to write down numbers and letters of the alphabet accurately.

11 Listen and circle the numbers you hear in 1–8.
1 40 / 14
2 639942 / 639442
3 5.15 / 5.50
4 £8.95 / £18.90
5 2.5 kilos / 25 kilos
6 March 9 / March 19
7 6.20 Euro / 62 Euro
8 1862 / 1872

12 Listen to the spelling and write the names of the cities. There is a space for each letter.
1 _ _ _ _ _ _ _ _ _
2 _ _ _ _ _ _ _
3 _ _ _ _ _ _ _ _
4 _ _ _ _ _
5 _ _ _ _ _ _ _ _ _
6 _ _ _ _ _ _ _ _ _ _

13 Now look at this post-it note. What type of information is missing?

Example
1 *a name*

> Mario
> Your cousin Tino phoned. He's arriving at 1 .... Airport on flight
> 2 .... (that's with Ryanair) at
> 3 .... tomorrow lunchtime. If you can't meet him there, can you phone his mobile (4 ....) tonight, if possible before 5 .... p.m.
> Jenny

6 Read the recording script and look at the first set of pictures again. Which picture goes with each underlined word?
  A Hi Anna. Is your brother Tomas playing <u>beach volleyball</u> with his friends this afternoon?
  B They really love doing that, but this morning they all got up late so they're at the <u>swimming pool</u> in town instead. It takes over an hour by bus to get to the <u>beach</u>.

7 Underline the words that give you the correct answer.

⦿ **PET Point**
In Listening Part 1, you will hear something about every picture in the set, so you must listen carefully!

8 Now listen to the recording for the other sets of pictures. Choose A or B to answer the questions.

Grammar

Present tenses

9 Write answers to the questions you chose in 4, using the pictures to help. Which present tenses have you used in answering 1 and 2? Why?

10 Now ask and answer questions 1–4 with a partner.
  1 What are you studying at the moment?
  2 Where do you live?
  3 How do you get to your English class?
  4 What are you doing after this lesson?

14 Listen and complete the sentences. You will hear the recording twice so don't worry if you don't complete everything the first time.

9

Writing 1 Thinking about your writing

Warm up

1 How much writing do you do? Tick (✓) what is true for you and then compare with a partner.

	In your language	In English
Sending text messages		
Answering emails		
Doing homework		
Making shopping lists		
Writing postcards		
Leaving notes for people		
Taking phone messages		
Writing letters to friends		
Writing formal letters		

● **PET Point**
Writing Part 1 is the one Writing task where both spelling and grammar must be 100% accurate.

Spelling words correctly

2 Correct the spelling errors in the PET level words in 1–8. One word in each pair is correct.

Example
photo   ~~fone~~   phone

1	beleive	receive
2	swiming	writing
3	beatiful	theatre
4	through	enought
5	middel	castle
6	definitly	immediately
7	teacher	docter
8	jaket	clock

Getting the grammar right

3 The *PET Masterclass* Grammar reference covers the grammar commonly tested in PET. Here are some of the important areas of grammar you will need to know for Writing Part 1. Add another example to each area.

Comparison	*as big as*
Conditional words	*unless*
Modal verbs	*mustn't*
Pronouns	*mine*
Quantifiers	*much*

4 Use the grammar words in 3 to complete the sentences. Then sort them into pairs of sentences with the same meaning.

1 You .... use your mobile phone here.
2 Jack is my friend.
3 We'll be hungry .... we have something to eat.
4 Your new apartment is not .... your old one.
5 Mobile phones are not allowed here.
6 We never take .... luggage on holiday.
7 If we don't eat something, we'll be hungry.
8 Your old apartment was bigger than your new one.
9 Jack is a friend of ....
10 We always travel light on holiday.

● **PET Point**
Don't just check your writing for spelling and grammar, look at word order and punctuation too.

Checking word order

5 In question 10 in 4, the adverb *always* cannot go in many different places in the sentence. Correct the word order in 1–6.

Questions

Example
What time it is?
What time is it?

1 How much that picture is?
2 Which colour you would like?
3 Who you did see at the concert?

Adverbs

I leave my mobile at home never.
I never leave my mobile at home.

4 People catch often fish here.
5 I bought yesterday a new bicycle.

Adjective order

6 There are ten red new chairs in our classroom.

Correcting punctuation

6 Read the text about the highest mountain in South America. Put in all the capital letters, full stops and commas needed.

Example
This is Cerro Aconcagua, the highest mountain outside the Himalayas.

this is cerro aconcagua the highest mountain outside the himalayas aconcagua is in the andes it is not difficult to climb if you are fit the normal route is just a steep path for most of the time some adventurous people even go up the path on motorbikes and bicycles the main problem is the cold at night which can be minus 40 degrees even in summer there are also dangerous storms on the mountain and the air is very thin experienced climbers know it is best not to hurry so they take a lot of food and water and climb slowly

7 Read the exam task. Decide which postcard, A or B, covers all three points. Then say which sentences in the postcard go with each point.

You are on holiday in another country and decide to send a postcard to your friend Sam.
In your postcard, you should

- tell Sam where you are staying
- explain what you like most about the holiday
- say what you did yesterday.

A

Dear Sam
I'm travelling around South America with some friends from college. This is the best holiday ever! Yesterday we flew over the Andes and we could see for miles from the plane. It was wonderful. See you when I get back.
Love from Gerry

B

Dear Sam
I'm spending three weeks in Chile, staying in different places up and down the coast. The best thing about Chile is the food. The fish here is really fresh. Yesterday we went out on a boat and caught our own lunch!
Love Lorenzo

● **PET Point**
In Writing Part 2 errors may not lower your mark, but you must communicate all three points in the task.

Using the *PET Masterclass* Vocabulary reference 1

Topic vocabulary

1 There are 20 words for parts of the body in this word square. See how many you can find. The words go ➔ or ⬇.

S	L	U	N	G	H	E	A	D	Y
H	A	N	K	L	E	Y	H	E	F
O	D	W	N	T	A	E	A	C	I
U	T	L	E	S	R	L	I	P	N
L	H	T	E	U	T	O	R	N	G
D	U	H	F	M	O	U	T	H	E
E	M	R	E	A	R	A	O	E	R
R	B	O	N	E	S	N	O	S	E
O	T	A	R	M	D	A	T	O	E
L	S	T	O	M	A	C	H	S	D

2 Now use the list of words on page 121 in *PET Masterclass* to complete and check your answers.

■ The *PET Masterclass* Vocabulary reference lists important words for every topic in PET.

3 Read descriptions 1–6 and choose other parts of the body from the list on page 121. One letter is given to help you.
1 It's inside your head and you use it to think.
   _ _ a _ _
2 You have this all over your body. _ k _ _
3 You wear boots or shoes on these. _ _ e _
4 This helps you to speak and taste food.
   _ o _ _ _ _
5 You hold a pen and write with this. _ _ _ d
6 This is red and goes round your body. _ _ o _ _

Verbs and nouns that go together

4 When you learn new vocabulary, it is sometimes a good idea to write down sets of words. For example, several verbs go with the word *clothes*.

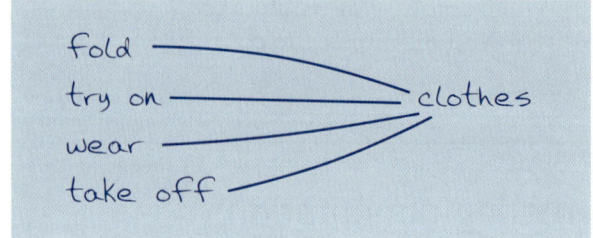

Choose a noun to go with each set of verbs.
Use each noun once only.

~~ankle~~   leg   lunch   door   jogging   train

Example
break   bruise   sprain   *ankle*

1 enjoy   go   start
2 lock   open   close
3 cut   hurt   injure
4 catch   get   take
5 cook   eat   have

5 Now use some of the verbs in **4** in the correct tense to complete the sentences. Sometimes you can use more than one verb.

Example
I …*went*… running three times last week.
1 What can we ……… for dinner? We only have potatoes and eggs.
2 Last year I ………… my arm in a fall – it was in plaster for six weeks.
3 Did you ………… the bathroom window before you left the house this morning?
4 How about ………… your black dress to the party?
5 We ………… plenty of fresh air yesterday because we walked all day.

■ In *PET Masterclass*, this sign ➔ **VOCABULARY REFERENCE PAGE 000** tells you when you can get help from the Vocabulary reference.

Using the PET Masterclass Grammar reference 1

■ The *PET Masterclass* Grammar reference covers all the grammar you need for PET!

Grammar terminology

1 Look at pages 126–127 in *PET Masterclass*. Find the grammar terminology.

base form   negative (sentence)   irregular verb
adjective   interrogative   regular verb   adverb
affirmative (sentence)   noun

2 Label 1–9 with the grammar terminology in **1**.

1 .... made
2 .... carefully
3 .... I didn't see Paul yesterday.
4 .... wanted
5 .... book
6 .... I play tennis every Tuesday.
7 .... have
8 .... expensive
9 .... Can you drive?

3 Find examples of the grammar terminology in the text.

> **What is the Grammar reference?**
> On pages 126–135 in PET Masterclass there is a Grammar reference section. It tells you about the grammar in each unit. There are short explanations and lots of examples. Read it slowly and use the examples to help you understand. Tell yourself – English grammar isn't difficult!

■ In *PET Masterclass*, this sign → **GRAMMAR REFERENCE PAGE 000** tells you when you can get help from the Grammar reference.

Verbs in the past simple

4 Correct any mistakes with the past tense verbs in the text. Use the *PET Masterclass* Grammar reference on pages 126–127 to help.

> **Top marks!**
>
> Shelley **1** wasn't know what to do. She **2** had to give her teacher an essay tomorrow morning. It **3** did be now 10p.m. and she **4** was tired. She **5** didn't wanted to stay up and work. So she **6** did phone her friend Kim to get some advice. Kim's marks **7** was very good this term. Shelley **8** knew she would help. She **9** was dialled Kim's number. After the phone call, Shelley **10** felt much better. She **11** did turn on her computer, and **12** started to work. By 11p.m. she **13** did be in bed listening to her favourite band on her iPod.

5 Complete the sentences with the correct past tense form of the verbs. Use the *PET Masterclass* Grammar reference on pages 126–127 to help

> She **14** .... (sleep) well, and **15** .... (get up) in good time for school. On the way, she **16** .... (buy) some chocolates to give Kim to thank her for the advice. She **17** .... (hand in) her essay and left the class feeling happy. It **18** .... (be) the weekend! The teacher **19** .... (spend) part of his weekend marking essays and on Monday afternoon he **20** .... (speak) to each student about their work. When he **21** .... (ask) Shelley to see him, he was smiling. 'He **22** .... (like) it!' Shelley **23** .... (think).

6 Complete the spaces with the correct past tense form of the verbs. Use the *PET Masterclass* Grammar reference on pages 126–127 to help.

give   say   not able to   write   be
not like   think

> 'This is an excellent piece of work, Shelley,' he **24** .... 'I've given it top marks. When I **25** .... it 20 years ago, my teacher **26** .... it and **27** .... me a low mark, but I always **28** .... it **29** .... much better than that. Of course, you **30** .... find other people's work on the internet in those days...'

13

Reading 2   Making connections

Warm up

1 Work with a partner. Tell each other what activities you do to keep fit.

Matching people to texts

2 Read the three descriptions of people and complete the table.

	Ride a bike	Swim	Other sports
Jane	✓	✓	
Kenny			
Megan			

Jane can ride a bike, and she can swim. She works at home during the week on her own and she's quite lonely.

Kenny cycles to work. His wife works in the evenings so he looks after the children. He loves football but he can't swim.

Megan goes to college in the mornings and has a part-time job as a cashier in a supermarket in the afternoons. She can't ride a bike but she likes swimming.

3 Jane, Kenny and Megan want to find a regular activity to keep fit. Read the texts below. Tick (✓) the activities with sports they can do.

1 **Aquafit**
Movement and music in the pool. Listen to the latest hits and keep fit. Every afternoon at 2p.m.

2 **RIDE & LUNCH CLUB**
Do you want to keep fit and meet people? Meet at 10.30 at the Newtown roundabout on Saturdays for a cycle ride and lunch.

3 **Dads' football**
Camphill Park, Sundays 10–12. Informal games. Bring the family and a picnic.

4 NOW OPEN **City Sports Centre**
Gym, squash courts, 50m swimming pool, running and cycle tracks and football pitches. Open till 9p.m. every day.

5 **PLAY FOOTBALL FOR NEWTOWN**
The team practises on Tuesday and Thursday evenings from 7.30–9.00 and plays matches on Sunday mornings. Phone Dave Collins on 01563 884712.

	1	2	3	4	5
Jane	✓	✓		✓	
Kenny					
Megan					

14

4 Now answer the questions.
1. Which activity can't Jane do because she's working?
2. Which of the other two activities is best for her? Why?
3. Kenny can't do two activities because he's babysitting. Which two?
4. Which of the other two activities is better for him? Why?
5. Do Megan's studies and job stop her from doing anything?
6. Which activity is best for her? Why?

● **PET Point**
In Reading Part 2 you have to match people to things and activities.

Fact or opinion?

5 Read the text about Will Stone who works as a personal trainer. What sports does he enjoy with his family?

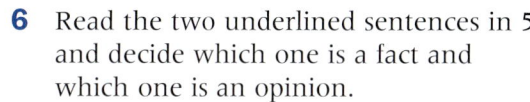

Healthy and happy

I think everyone needs to know the things that keep them happy. For me, it's food, exercise and my family. I love eating, but I'm careful what I eat. Generally, I eat healthy foods, such as fish or salads. If I have cakes or biscuits, I feel sleepy and can't concentrate. For me it's important in my job to be able to give advice about a healthy diet as well as keeping fit. Although I work with people who want to keep fit, I don't always get the exercise I need. So I go for a run in the evening and go for a long bike ride at the weekend. We live on the edge of town, so I can get out into the countryside very quickly.

My wife and children also like sports and outdoor activities. We have a lot of fun together cycling, swimming and sailing. In my opinion one of the most important lessons you can teach young people is how to be healthy.

6 Read the two underlined sentences in **5** and decide which one is a fact and which one is an opinion.

7 Complete the sentences with *fact* and *opinion*.
1. A(n) ………….. gives you information about something.
2. A(n) ………….. tells you what somebody thinks about something.

8 Underline two more opinions Will Stone gives in the article, and find three more facts about him.

● **PET Point**
In Reading Part 4 you answer questions on a text which gives the writer's opinion about something.

Grammar
Ability

9 Complete the sentences.

Example
Megan ………… (can ✓) go to the sports centre in the evenings.
Megan *can* go to the sports centre in the evenings.

1. Kenny ………….. (can ✓) ride a bike, but he (be able to ✗)………….. swim.
2. Jane ………….. (be able to ✗) to go to Aquafit because she works in the afternoon.
3. Will and his family ……………. (be able to ✓) enjoy keeping fit together.
4. Kenny ………… (can ✗) play football for the Newtown team.
5. Megan ………… (be able to ✓) swim, but she (can ✗) ………… ride a bike.
6. Will …………….. (can ✓) run or cycle in the countryside, because he lives on the edge of town.

10 In pairs, tell each other which of the activities in **3** you can and can't do. Which activity do you like best?

Speaking 2 Making choices

Warm up

1 In pairs, tell each other which of the holidays you would like best and why.

Making suggestions

2 Two people are talking about their friend, Polly. Use the phrases to complete the dialogue.

How about   I think   She could   ~~What do you think~~   Maybe she'd

Tanya I spoke to Polly last night. She's much better. She's going on holiday. Did she tell you?
Greg No, but it's a good idea. Where's she going?
Tanya She doesn't know. *What do you think* she should do?
Greg 1............ go on a coach tour. She likes meeting people, and someone else does all the driving.
Tanya Yes, but travelling every day can make you very tired. 2.............. she needs something more exciting, like a trip to Africa to see wild animals. You don't travel very far every day, and it's a completely new experience.
Greg Yes, it is, but there's the long flight to get there, and it might be very hot and dusty. 3............... a beach and water sports holiday? She loves swimming.
Tanya That's true. She could swim or relax on the beach, but I don't think she's got the energy for windsurfing or sailing at the moment. 4................ like to spend a few days exploring a city? She could go sightseeing or just sit in cafés.

3 Listen and check your answers.

4 Read and listen to the rest of the dialogue. Which holiday do they decide is best for Polly?

Greg It's a bit boring on your own, though. Why don't we advise her to go to the mountains? They're so beautiful at this time of year. She can sit and look at the view, or go for short walks. What do you think?
Tanya I think that's a great idea. She can read or just relax in the beautiful countryside. Let's talk to her about it.

5 Underline two more ways of making suggestions in 4.

● **PET Point**
In Speaking Part 2 you have a discussion and make a decision with another candidate.

Making decisions

9 Your friend, Ben, is in hospital. You are going to visit him and want to take something for him. Label the presents.

Agreeing and disagreeing

6 Tanya and Greg agree (A) and disagree (D) with each other during their conversation. Find these phrases in the dialogue and write A or D next to each one.
1 I think that's a great idea. ……..
2 Yes, but… …….
3 That's true. …….
4 Yes it is, but… …….

Giving reasons

7 When Tanya and Greg reply to each other's suggestions, they give reasons why they agree or disagree. Answer the questions.
1 Who says a coach tour can be very tiring?
2 Why does Tanya think water sports are not a good idea?
3 What does Greg say about the trip to Africa?
4 What are Tanya's reasons for suggesting Polly visits a city?
5 Why do they think a trip to the mountains is the best holiday? Find five reasons.

8 In pairs, think of more reasons why Polly should or shouldn't go on the different holidays. Use this language to help.

A I think Polly should ………… because ………. .
B Yes, but ………….. .
A I think she should …………….. because ………. .
B Yes, that's true. She can also ………………. .

10 On your own make some notes. Write one reason why each present is a good choice and one reason why each present is not suitable.

Example
CDs + *You can play them and not hear the noise around you.*
      – *He might not have a CD player in hospital.*

11 In pairs, talk about the presents. Decide which present would be the best to take Ben. Use phrases in Tanya's and Greg's dialogue to help you.

● **PET Point**
In Speaking Part 2 agree and disagree with your partner's suggestions and give reasons.

Listening 2 Hearing about thoughts and feelings

Warm up

1 Work with a partner. Decide which sentences are about the iPod advert and which ones are about the Mercedes advert.
  1 I'm sure you can see this billboard from a long way away – it's huge!
  2 Using only a few colours is great, especially the black on pink.
  3 There's so much to read in the advert.
  4 The message is very clear without lots of words.
  5 This advert is aimed at older people.
  6 It's interesting with all those pictures behind the product.
  7 That big black capital letter must be because of its name.
  8 The image is very strong – you can almost hear the music!

2 Work with a partner. Compare the advertisements and decide
  • which advert is more attractive and why.
  • which advert is better at selling the product and why.

3 Describe your favourite advertisement. Why do you like it?

Understanding people's opinions

● **PET Point**
In Listening Part 4, two people discuss their feelings, thoughts or opinions.

4 You will hear some people talking about the advertisements above. Decide what each person thinks about each advertisement and choose ☺ or ☹.

	iPod advert		Mercedes advert	
Chris	☺	☹	☺	☹
Anna	☺	☹	☺	☹
David	☺	☹	☺	☹
Lourdes	☺	☹	☺	☹
José	☺	☹	☺	☹
Maria	☺	☹	☺	☹

5 Check you understand the adjectives below. Then listen and choose one adjective to describe how each person feels. One adjective isn't used.

angry   bored   confident   disappointed   pleased   surprised   worried

1 Emma   ....
2 Nick   ....
3 Cathy   ....
4 Ben   ....
5 Helen   ....
6 Jack   ....

● **PET Point**
Each Listening Part 2 question has three possible answers, A, B or C. You will hear information about all three.

6 Read the question and match the three speech bubbles to A, B and C. Which words help you to do this?

How does Ken feel about his job in the advertising agency?

A bored by the work he is doing
B pleased at the success of his ideas
C less worried than he was at the beginning

1 It's great to see that the things I was thinking about only two months ago are in advertisements already.

2 There were a lot of new things to learn when I joined the company, but it's a bit easier now.

3 I'm disappointed actually, because at the moment every day is the same, and the work is really dull.

7 Now listen to what Ken actually said. Answer the question in **5**, choosing A, B or C.

8 Underline the words in the recording script that support your choice of answer. Have you answered the question correctly?

Well, I only joined two months ago so it's too early to see any of my ideas in finished advertisements. It's fun at work though and no two days are the same, which is great. I also feel a bit more confident now because I'm not new any more. It was hard at first.

9 Now look at the other two choices in **5**. Underline the words in the recording script that go with them.

● **PET Point**
Every Listening task will include words to suggest wrong answers, so listen carefully!

Grammar
Comparison

10 Complete the sentences about the advertisements using a comparative form of the adjective in brackets. Then talk about the billboard below.

Example

The iPod advert *is easier* (easy) to understand than the car advert.

1 The iPod advert seems .... (strong) than the Mercedes advert.
2 The iPod advert is .... (suitable) for young people than the Mercedes advert.
3 The Mercedes advert feels .... (complicated) than the iPod advert.
4 The Mercedes advert uses a .... (wide) range of colours than the iPod advert.

Writing 2 Developing your writing

Warm up

1. Do you enjoy writing or telling stories? Why? / Why not?

2. Look at the picture story. In pairs, say what is happening in each picture.

3. How does the girl feel in picture 6, do you think? What will she do next?

● **PET Point**
Writing Part 3, which is a choice between a story and a letter, carries 60% of the Writing marks. To score high marks, you need to use a good variety of language and long sentences.

Writing longer sentences

4 Join the pairs of sentences. Use the words in brackets and make any changes necessary.

Example
It was dark. Anna got up. (when)
It was dark when Anna got up.

1. She packed her rucksack. She waited for a taxi. (and then)
2. The taxi arrived. Anna got in. (and)
3. It took her to the station. She was catching a train for Manchester. (because)
4. Anna got on to a train. She didn't check its destination. (but)
5. Anna fell asleep. She felt tired. (because)
6. A ticket collector woke her. He asked to see her ticket. (and)

5 Now add the words to the sentences in 4 to make them longer and more complex.

Example
It was still dark when Anna got up.

in a hurry   soon   main
stupidly   extremely   up   ~~still~~

Showing vocabulary range

6 Read the next part of the story and use the words to complete the sentences.

miserable   nastily   off   really
suddenly   wrong

> The ticket collector told her quite
> 1 .... that she was on the 2 ....
> train. Anna was 3 .... surprised
> and a bit annoyed with herself. She got
> 4 .... the train at the next station
> and found a place to sit down, feeling
> rather 5 .... But then she 6 ....
> saw a boy she knew from college.

● **PET Point**
Learn new words and phrases like these and use them to impress the examiners!

Showing grammatical range

7 Read the rest of the story. The boxes show you some of the grammar areas you will be covering in *PET Masterclass*.

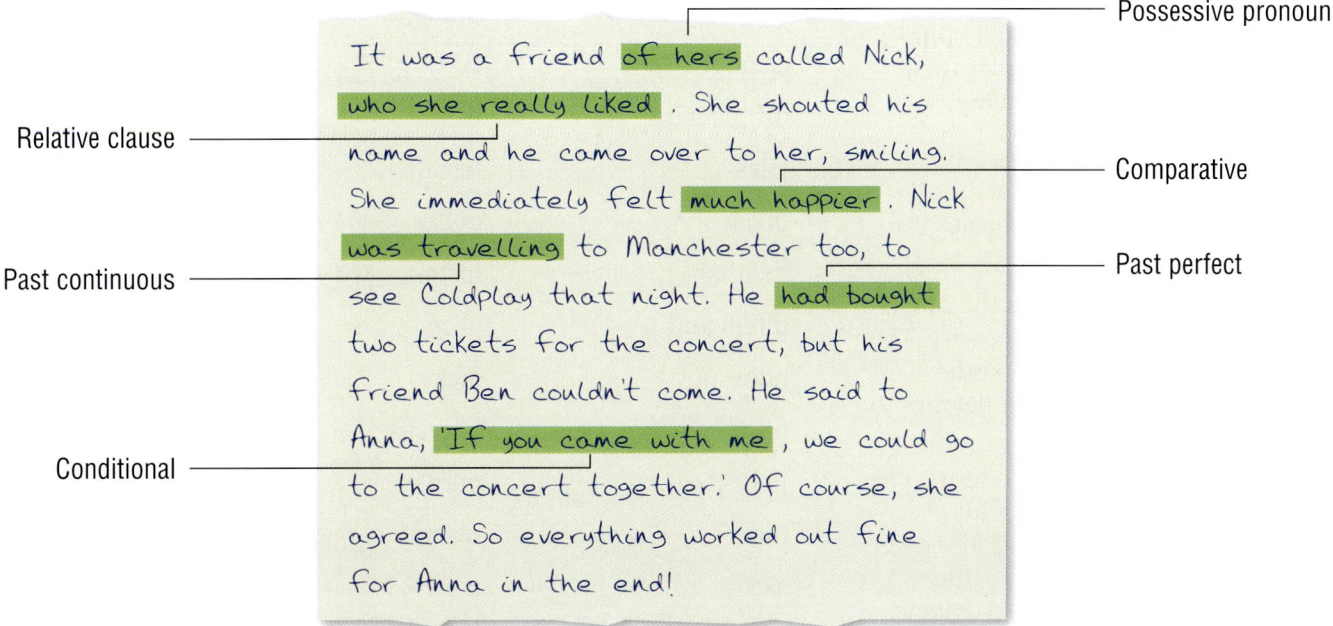

● **PET Point**
To write a Part 3 story, you need to know the past tenses of a lot of verbs. In Unit 1 of the Grammar reference for *PET Masterclass*, there is a list of PET level irregular verbs. Practise using them correctly.

Using the *PET Masterclass* **Vocabulary reference 2**

Describing things

1 Write the names for the clothes. Check the list on page 121 of *PET Masterclass* if you need to.

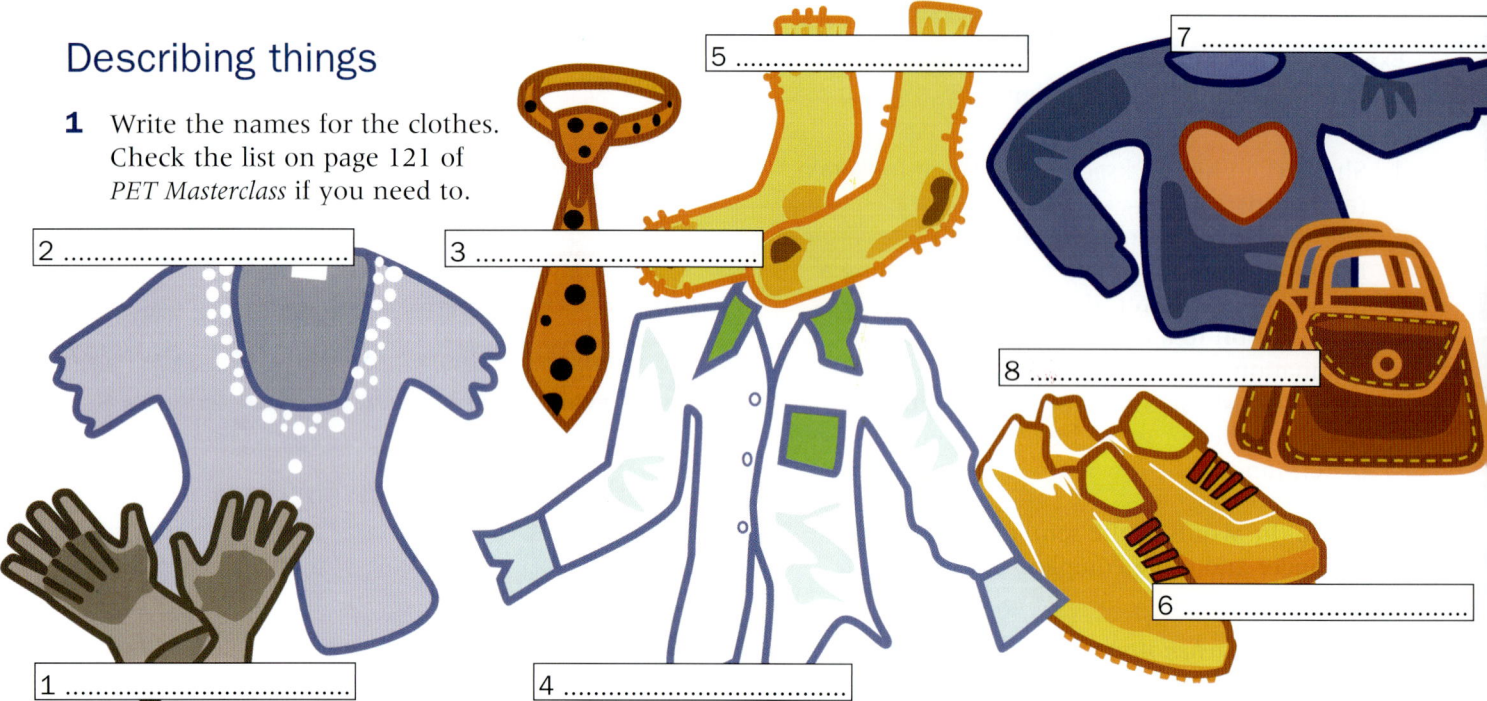

2 Use adjectives from the list on page 122 to describe the clothes.

Example
a dark blue jumper with a large pink heart

3 Now use both lists to write phrases to describe what other students in your class are wearing today. Tell your partner your phrases and let them guess who you are describing.

● **PET Point**
Use different adjectives in the speaking test and in your writing, to impress the examiners!

4 Decide which adjective is the odd one out in the sets and explain why. Then find a word on page 122 of the Vocabulary reference that belongs to the same set.

1 ancient   antique   modern   old
2 broad   large   tiny   wide
3 blue   blue-grey   blueish   green
4 damp   warm   sunny   fine
5 glass   leather   silk   woollen

5 The adjectives below could be tested in PET. Using a dictionary to check meaning if necessary, write a noun that goes with each one. Use the Vocabulary reference to give you some ideas.

angry	....	attractive	....	bare	....
bitter	....	brilliant	....	cheap	....
cloudy	....	curly	....	direct	....
disgusting	....	easy	....	enormous	....
false	....	female	....	funny	....
good	....	guilty	....	hard	....
healthy	....	historic	....	icy	....
intelligent	....	juicy	....	keen	....
little	....	lucky	....	mad	....
nasty	....	nervous	....	ordinary	....
perfect	....	purple	....	quiet	....
rare	....	roast	....	scientific	....
sick	....	smart	....	special	....
tasty	....	terrible	....	unleaded	....
untidy	....	useful	....	various	....
warm	....	well-made	....	wild	....

Using the PET Masterclass Grammar reference 2

Grammar – form

■ The *form* of the grammar is the words you put together and how they change.

1 Turn to page 127 in the Grammar reference in *PET Masterclass*. Use the information in the table on page 127 about how to make comparisons to complete the table below.

Adjective	Comparative	Superlative
Single syllable *small*		
Two syllables ending in *-y* *happy*		
Two syllables ending in *-ful*, or *-ly* *thoughtful*		
Three or more syllables *interesting*		

2 Study the table about ability at the top of page 128. Underline the verbs in sentences 1–6 which show ability. Then match them to the grammar terminology.

Past affirmative   Future negative
Present negative   Future affirmative
Past negative   Present affirmative

1 Peter can speak French and Italian.
2 Clare couldn't find her front door key.
3 I'll be able to visit you very often.
4 Oliver can't drive yet – he's only 16.
5 They won't be able to come to the party.
6 Sharon was able to ski well at the end of the week.

Grammar – use

■ In the Grammar reference, sentences starting *We use…* tell you when to use a grammar point.

3 Read the explanation about imperatives on page 128. When do we use the imperative? Tick (✓) the situations.

to thank people   to tell somebody what to do
to make suggestions   to give information
to give warnings   to give instructions
to make a request   to make an offer
to give directions   to give advice

4 Read about the uses of the past simple and continuous on page 127. Write the uses under the correct heading.

past states   activities in progress at a particular time in the past   things that happened in the past   temporary situations in the past
a situation in the past that is interrupted by an action or event   past habits

Past simple	Past continuous
We use the past simple to talk about …	We use the past continuous to talk about …

5 Read the explanation about *some* and *any* on page 126. Match 1–6 with example sentences a–f.

1 Negative sentences
2 Affirmative sentences to talk about a quantity (with uncountable nouns)
3 Most questions
4 Affirmative sentences to talk about a number (with countable nouns)
5 Questions which make a request
6 Questions which make an offer

a Have you got any stamps?
b There weren't any peaches in the market.
c Would you like some tea?
d We've got some homework to do this evening.
e Could you give me some information about hotels?
f I need some new shoes.

■ In *PET Masterclass*, this SEE UNIT 2 FOR COMPARISON OF ADVERBS sign tells you there's more information about this grammar point in another part of the Grammar reference.

OXFORD
UNIVERSITY PRESS

Great Clarendon Street, Oxford OX2 6DP

Oxford University Press is a department of the University of Oxford.
It furthers the University's objective of excellence in research, scholarship,
and education by publishing worldwide in

Oxford   New York

Auckland Cape Town Dar es Salaam Hong Kong Karachi
Kuala Lumpur Madrid Melbourne Mexico City Nairobi
New Delhi Shanghai Taipei Toronto

With offices in

Argentina Austria Brazil Chile Czech Republic France Greece
Guatemala Hungary Italy Japan Poland Portugal Singapore
South Korea Switzerland Thailand Turkey Ukraine Vietnam

OXFORD and OXFORD ENGLISH are registered trade marks of
Oxford University Press in the UK and in certain other countries

© Oxford University Press 2006

The moral rights of the author have been asserted

Database right Oxford University Press (maker)

First published 2006

2011 2010 2009 2008
10 9 8 7 6

No unauthorized photocopying

All rights reserved. No part of this publication may be reproduced,
stored in a retrieval system, or transmitted, in any form or by any means,
without the prior permission in writing of Oxford University Press,
or as expressly permitted by law, or under terms agreed with the appropriate
reprographics rights organization. Enquiries concerning reproduction
outside the scope of the above should be sent to the ELT Rights Department,
Oxford University Press, at the address above

You must not circulate this book in any other binding or cover
and you must impose this same condition on any acquirer

Any websites referred to in this publication are in the public domain and
their addresses are provided by Oxford University Press for information only.
Oxford University Press disclaims any responsibility for the content

ISBN: 978 0 19 451407 1

Printed in China

ACKNOWLEDGEMENTS

The authors and publisher would like to thank the following for permission to reproduce photographs: Alamy p11 (Herbert Scholpp/Westend61); iStockphoto pp14bc (Tobias Lauchenauer), 14tc (Anna Bryukhanova); Linographic pp14b, 15; Mercedes-Benz (UK) Ltd./DaimlerChrysler UK Ltd p18l; Powells Cottage Holidays p7; Rex Features p18r (Peter Brooker). OUP pp4 (girl with mobile), 19 (Milan/Robert Mullan).

Illustrations by: Spike Gerrell pp5, 13, 20, 23; Mark Duffin pp7, 10, 14, 16, 17; Tim Kahane pp8, 9, 22.